ULTIMATE
PUZZLE CHALLENGE

By
Helene Hovanec

Illustr
Matt

D1042576

STERLING

New York / London
www.sterlingpublishing.com/kids

STERLING and the distinctive Sterling logo are registered trademarks of Sterling Publishing Co., Inc.

Lot #: 10 9 8 7 6 5 4 3
05/12
Published by Sterling Publishing Co., Inc.
387 Park Avenue South, New York, NY 10016
© 2009 by Helene Hovanec
Illustrations © 2009 by Matt Luxich
Distributed in Canada by Sterling Publishing
c/o Canadian Manda Group, 165 Dufferin Street
Toronto, Ontario, Canada M6K 3H6
Distributed in the United Kingdom by GMC Distribution Services
Castle Place, 166 High Street, Lewes, East Sussex, England BN7 1XU
Distributed in Australia by Capricorn Link (Australia) Pty. Ltd.
P.O. Box 704, Windsor, NSW 2756, Australia

Sterling ISBN 978-1-4027-6204-8

For information about custom editions, special sales, premium and corporate purchases, please contact Sterling Special Sales Department at 800-805-5489 or specialsales@sterlingpublishing.com.

INTRODUCTION

Welcome to the **Ultimate Puzzle Challenge**—a brand-new series of books for children who love word searches, crisscrosses, mazes, crosswords, and variety puzzles. As an added bonus, many puzzles are based on silly riddles that will make you giggle or smile.

I hope **Mind Mashers** will amuse and challenge you at the same time. You may whiz through some puzzles in just a few minutes, but others might make your brain work overtime. There are no rules to follow except the directions before each puzzle, so go through the book at your own pace. If you don't know something, it's okay to ask for help, use a dictionary, or even peek at the answer—these are all good ways to learn! The main goal is to have fun and exercise your brain.

Take the **Ultimate Puzzle Challenge** . . . and enjoy!

—Helene Hovanec

OPTICAL CONFUSION

How fast can you find five grids that are
exactly like this one?

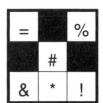

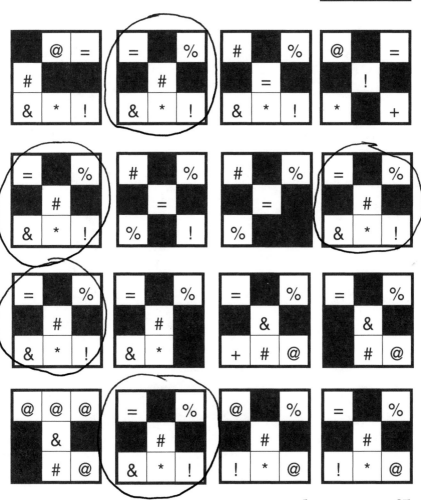

Answer on page 85.

FRONT OF THE LINE

Answer each clue with a five-letter word and write it in the blanks. Then, when you have all the blanks filled in, read down the first column to answer this riddle:
Why did the waiter fall over?

Clue	Answer
Word said when you answer the phone	H e l l o
The number before nine	E i g h t
Adult females	W o m e n
The fourth month	A p r i l
Tomato-lettuce-cucumber dish	S a l a d
"___ or treat?" (Halloween phrase)	T r i c k
Presses clothes	I r o n s
Dish	P l a t e
Opposite of war	P e a c e
Our planet	E a r t h
Quacking birds	D u c k s

Answers on page 87.

THE NAME GAME

Place one boy's name from the box into the blank spaces on each line to form a word that fits the clue.

> ~~ABE~~   ~~BEN~~   ~~DAN~~   ~~GIL~~
>
> ~~IRA~~   ~~KEN~~
>
> ~~LEN~~   ~~LOU~~   ~~MEL~~   SAM

1. Delicate — FRA <u>G I L</u> E
2. Girl's clothing item — B <u>L O U</u> S E
3. More than enough — P L <u>E N</u> T Y
4. Identifying tag — L A B E L
5. Something chewy and sweet — C A R A <u>M E L</u>
6. Saturday and Sunday — W E E <u>K E N</u> D
7. Famous TV "Street" — S E S <u>A M</u> E
8. Extraordinary event — M <u>I R A</u> C L E
9. Under — <u>B E N</u> E A T H
10. Risky — <u>D A N</u> G E R O U S

Answers on page 86.

ADD-A-LETTER

Add one letter to each line and rearrange the letters to make words that answer the clues.

A

M A	Pa's wife
A R M	Shoulder-wrist connector
M A R S	Fourth planet from the sun
M A R E S	Female horses
S T R E A M	Small body of water
H A M S T E R	Rodent with cheek pouches

THIS AUTO BE FUN

Draw a line between the car in the left column and its driver in the right column.

Answers on page 85.

LAZY BONES

Put each word into the grid on the opposite page in alphabetical order. Read down the starred column to answer this riddle: What do you call a lazy kangaroo?

PASTURE

PELICAN

POSTAGE

PACE

PINCH

PLUMP

POET

PRINTER

PROOF

PARROT

PAPER

PORT

		*		
	P	A	C	E
	P	A	P	E	R

P	A	R	R	O	T
P	A	S	T	U	R	E
P	E	L	I	C	A	N
P	I	N	C	H

P	L	U	M	P
P	O	E	T
P	O	R	T
P	O	S	T	A	G	E
P	R	I	N	T	E	R
P	R	O	O	F

Answers on page 85.

MAGIC SQUARES

In a magic square, the answer words are the same both **ACROSS** and **DOWN**. So, answer each clue with a four-letter word and put it in the grid both ways. We did the first one for you.

✓ 1. Closed
✓ 2. Wish (for)
✓ 3. "Once ___ a time"
✓ 4. Camper's "house"

	1	2	3	4
1	S	H	U	T
2	H	O	P	E
3	U	P	O	N
4	T	E	N	T

A

✓ 1. Not healthy
✓ 2. Device for pressing clothes
✓ 3. Ice cream holder
✓ 4. Recognized

	1	2	3	4
1	S	I	C	K
2	I	R	O	N
3	C	O	N	E
4	K	N	E	W

B

1. Opposite of work
2. The opposite of find
3. The largest continent
4. A 365-day period

	1	2	3	4
1	P	L	A	Y
2	L	O	S	E
3	A	S	I	A
4	Y	E	A	R

C

1. Coins and bills
2. Type of code for phoning
3. Opposite of buy
4. Fifty percent

	1	2	3	4
1	C	A	S	H
2	A	R	E	A
3	S	E	L	L
4	H	A	L	F

D

Answers on page 86.

TEACHER'S PET

Read each clue and cross off its definition on the opposite page. Then write the leftover words, from left to right and top to bottom, on the line. They won't make any sense. But . . . change the first letter in each word to answer this riddle: What do you get when you cross a vampire and a teacher?

CLUES

✓ 1. Act like a pilot
✓ 2. Computer problem
✓ 3. Belly
✓ 4. Someone who's tardy
✓ 5. Worry
✓ 6. Ending
✓ 7. Fight
✓ 8. Imitated a turkey
✓ 9. Person who lives on our planet
✓ 10. Odd
✓ 11. Western riding event
✓ 12. Additional
✓ 13. Prize
✓ 14. Where you sit down
✓ 15. Cleaning tool
✓ 16. Type of dance

~~STOMACH~~	~~AWARD~~	POTS	~~BATTLE~~
~~RODEO~~	IF	~~VACUUM~~	FLOOD
~~GOBBLED~~	~~CONCLUSION~~	~~EARTHLING~~	~~FLY~~
~~VIRUS~~	~~EXTRA~~	~~STRESS~~	~~STRANGE~~
RESTS	~~WALTZ~~	~~COUCH~~	~~LATECOMER~~

Leftover words: <u>Pots If Flood Rests</u>

Change the first letter in
each word: <u>Lots Of Blood Tests</u>

Answers on page 87.

FOOD FIGHT

Circle nine differences between the picture on this page and the picture on the opposite page.

Answers on page 86.

THE "A" LIST

All of these words contain the letter "A." Put each word in its correct space in the grid. Start with the given letters and work from there until the grid is complete.

3 Letters
ART
MAN
SPA
TAB

4 Letters
DATA
FLAW
LAVA
MALL
PAPA
STAB
YAMS

5 Letters
LLAMA
WHARF

6 Letters
BANANA
CABANA
PAPAYA

7 Letters
ALABAMA
FARAWAY

8 Letters
MARYLAND

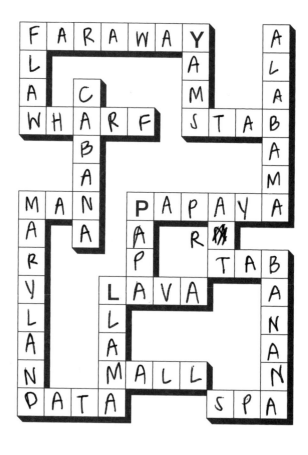

Answers on page 89.

DUMB THUMB

Answer each clue with a two-word rhyming phrase. Use the number of letters in each word and the clue letters to guide you.   **Example:** Large farm animal = BIG PIG

1. Ship jacket   B _ _ _   C _ _ _ _
2. Path for a walking aid   _ _ _ _   L _ _ _ _
3. Seasonal jewelry   _ _ _ _ _ G   _ _ _ _ _
4. Rodent's home   _ _ _ S _ _   _ _ _ _ _ _
5. Eating utensil for meat   _ O _ _ _   _ _ _ _ _
6. Carpet insect   R _ _ _   _ _ _ _
7. Dull-colored pottery material   _ _ _ A _ _   _ _ _ _ Y
8. Fine lumber   _ _ _ _ _   _ _ _ _ D
9. An even number of guys   _ _ _ _   M _ _ _
10. Comical baby rabbit   _ _ N _ _ _   _ _ _ _ _ _

Now, fill in the numbered blanks with your rhymes to read a nonsense story.

The _____ put on a _____ and
       [10]   [1]

a _____ and walked down the _____
    [3]   [2]

to the _____ which was made of _____
      [4]   [7]

and_____. There he saw _____
    [8]   [9]

hoping to use a _____ on a baked ham.
          [5]

Unfortunately, the _____ had already finished it!
         [6]

Answers on page 88.

BODY LANGUAGE

Place a three-letter body part into each set of blanks to make a word that answers the clue.

1. __ __ __ E N D   Folk story

2. P H __ __ __ A C Y   Drug store

3. P O P __ __ __   Sailor who loves spinach

4. T __ __ __ I N G   Ripping

5. S T A R S __ __ __   Science fiction vehicle

6. S __ __ __ P E R S   Comfy footwear for

   the house

7. P O T A __ __ __ S   Spuds

VACATION SPOT

Write a letter in each blank space to name a veggie. Then read down the column to find the three-word phrase that answers this riddle: Where do veggies stay on vacation?

```
        _ U R N I P
  R A D I S _
        L _ E K
      C E _ E R Y
        P _ P P E R
C A R R O _
      A R _ I C H O K E
      S Q _ A S H
        _ A U L I F L O W E R
C A B B A G _
      O N _ O N
    C O R _
      S P I _ A C H
```

Answers on page 90.

STEP BY STEP

To find a riddle and its answer, start at the circled letter in the grid and move one square at a time. Go straight across, up, or down, but *not* diagonally. Write each letter in the blanks to the right of the grid, and then cross it off in the grid as you use it. All letters and symbols in the grid will be used once.

A	T	.
H	H	E
W	O	G
D	L	N
S	W	O
T	A	P
E	A	S
R	?	S
B	L	E
U	O	H
T	O	F
I	L	L
S	F	U

W h a t _ _ _ _ _ _

_ _ _ _ _ _ _ _ _ _ _ _

_ _ _ _ _ _ _ _ _ _ _ _ _?

_ _ _ _ _ _ _ _ _ .

Answer on page 91.

A-MAZE-ING PATH

How fast can you get through this spider maze?

START

END

Answer on page 88.

RIDDLE CROSSWORD

Answer each clue and write it in the grid, either **ACROSS** or **DOWN**. Then fill in the numbered blanks below the grid with the letters in the numbered squares. Read the letters to answer this riddle: What did the dentist say when his wife baked a pie?

ACROSS

1. Between eighth and tenth
4. Grease
6. Group game, ___ of war
7. The country where New Delhi is located
8. Received
9. Cooling device
11. A person who is breathing is ___
13. Frozen water
15. A 24-hour period
16. The opposite of winner

DOWN

1. This divides a tennis court
2. Evening
3. The stuff that grows on your head
4. Ancient
5. Get some knowledge
8. Baby ___ piano
9. Travels by airplane
10. Type of phone
12. Rash, poison ___
14. Hearing organ

Answer:

$\overline{10}\ \overline{11}\ \overline{1}\quad \overline{13}\quad \overline{15}\ \overline{4}\quad \overline{6}\ \overline{3}\ \overline{14}\quad \overline{9}\ \overline{7}\ \overline{5}\ \overline{16}\ \overline{12}\ \overline{2}\ \overline{8}$?

Answers on page 89.

EMERGENCY!

Answer each clue and write the letters in the blanks. Then, move each letter to the same-numbered blank in the box on the opposite page. Work back and forth between the clues and the answer box. When all the letters have been filled in, read from 1 to 44 to find a riddle and answer.

1. The building in which you live

    __ __ __ __ __
    1 5 39 26 23

2. Had a meal

    __ __ __
    8 29 17

3. What a postal worker delivers

    __ __ __ __
    37 41 32 31

4. Opposite of front

    __ __ __ __
    38 30 43 12

5. Browned breakfast bread

    __ __ __ __ __
    18 2 34 9 19

6. Farm animal with horns

    __ __ __ __
    16 25 36 21

7. Potato ___ (snack foods)

    __ __ __ __ __
    11 24 14 27 7

8. Be of assistance to

           __ __ __ __
22 6 40 13

9. The number after eight

           __ __ __ __
42 10 33 44

10. Use a shovel

           __ __ __
4 28 15

11. Which person?

           __ __ __
3 35 20

__ __ __   __ __ __ __   __   __ __ __ __   __ __ __
1 2 3   4 5 6 7   8   9 10 11 12   13 14 15

__ __ __   __ __   __ __ __   __ __ __ __ __ __ __ __?
16 17 18   19 20   21 22 23   24 25 26 27 28 29 30 31

__ __   __   __ __ __ - __ __ __ __ __ __ __.
32 33   34   35 36 37 38 39 40 41 42 43 44

Answers on page 90.

SOUND OFF

Fill in the grid with words that sound like the listed words but have different meanings and are spelled differently. Then read **DOWN** the third column to find a three-word phrase that means "keep silent" or "don't tell anyone about this." The first one has been done for you.

1. HIM

2. WOOD

3. MIST

4. ROWS

5. ATE

6. CHOOSE

7. DAYS

8. SUITE

9. THROWN

10. WEAR

11. MAID

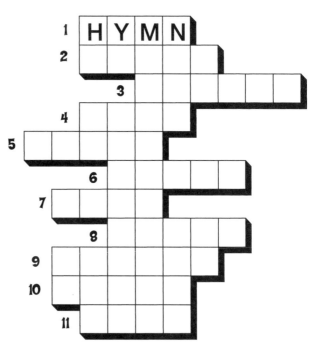

Answers on page 90.

CATCH OF THE DAY

All the answers here are in plain sight. Cross out some letters from the seafood in the left column to form a new word that answers the clue in the middle column. Do not change the order of the letters. The first one has been done to get you going.

1.	S A̷ L̷ M̷ O N	Male child	**SON**
2.	SMELT	Ran into	_____
3.	BLUEFISH	Turn red	_____
4.	PRAWN	Cooking utensil	_____
5.	CORAL	Heating fuel	_____
6.	SARDINE	Unhappy	_____
7.	FLOUNDER	Not against	_____
8.	SHRIMP	That guy	_____
9.	STURGEON	Heavy weight	_____
10.	ESCARGOT	Used a chair	_____
11.	HALIBUT	Small house	_____
12.	TURBOT	Bathing spot	_____

Answers on page 91.

WHR HV LL TH VWLS GN?

The letters A, E, I, O, U, and Y have been eliminated from the words below. Fill them back in to identify ten fairy tales.

1. THGLDCKLNG _____

2. CNDRLL _____

3. THLTTLMRMD _____

4. SLPNGBT _____

5. RMPLSTLTSKN _____

6. BTNDTHBST _____

7. RPNZL _____

8. THMPRRSNWCLTHS _____

9. SNWWHT _____

10. HNSLNDGRTL _____

Answers on page 90.

AUTHOR! AUTHOR!

Match each "author" with his or her book

AUTHOR

Cal Q. Later

Al Asker

A. Braine

J. Walker

Ken Dell Styx

N. E. Buddy

May O. Naze

K. C. Dilla

Gil Tee

Otto Moe Bill

BOOK

Answers on page 89.

DEAL ME OUT

Find and circle in the word search grid the eighteen card terms in the list below. Look up, down, and diagonally, both forward and backward. Then, take the leftover letters in the grid from left to right and top to bottom, and write them in the blanks on the facing page to answer this riddle: Why can't you play cards in the jungle?

ACE
CLUBS
DEAL
DECK
DEUCE
DIAMONDS
GO FISH
HEARTS
JACK
JOKER
KING
OLD MAID
PLAYERS
QUEEN
RULES
SOLITAIRE
SUIT
SPADES

```
B S O L I T A I R E E
E C S A N A O G S S
U S E E O L O T D E
F T E D D F R T N L
H U E M I A C I O U
Q H A S E C P U M R
E I H H B E E S A E
D E U C E U G N I K
T S R E Y A L P D O
A H S D E C K C A J
```

Answer: _ _ _ _ _ _ _ _   _ _   _ _ _

_ _ _ _ _ _ _ _ _

Answers on page 91.

PICTURE CROSSWORD

Name each picture and write it in the numbered space going **ACROSS** or **DOWN**.

ACROSS

1.

3.

6.

7.

9.

11.

12.

14.

17.

18.

19.

21.

22.

DOWN

1.

2.

3.

4.

5.

8.

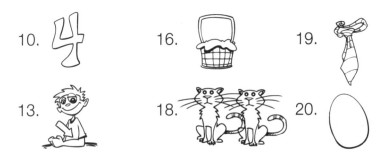

10.

16.

19.

13.

18.

20.

15.

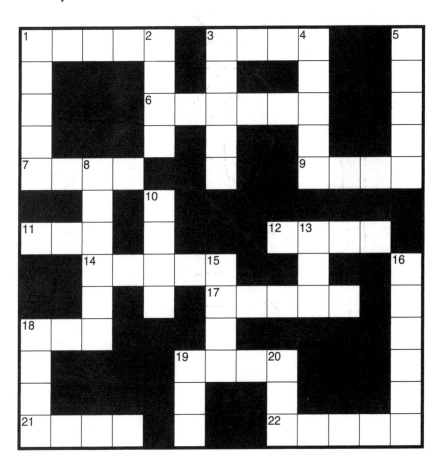

Answers on page 91.

CLOSE RELATIVES

Change just one letter in each word to make three
related words in each group. Don't change the order of
the letters.
Example: ROD, WHINE, and GLUE can be changed to
RED, WHITE, and BLUE. Use the hint at the top of each
word group to guide you.

1. **Meal Time**
   WINNER   _____
   SIPPER   _____
   BRANCH   _____

2. **On Your Feet**
   SHOWS   _____
   HOOTS   _____
   VANDALS   _____

3. **In the Family**
   BOTHER   _____
   FATTER   _____
   SITTER   _____

4. **Bodies of Water**
   BAKE   _____
   LIVER   _____
   PONY   _____

5. On Your Face
EVES   _____

CARS   _____

POSE   _____

6. In the House
SABLE   _____

CHAIN   _____

COACH   _____

7. Meats
STEAM   _____

DEAL   _____

PARK   _____

8. Drink It Up
TEN   _____

SILK   _____

SOFA   _____

9. What's Your Number?
FIX   _____

FIGHT   _____

FIRE   _____

10. Put It On
SWEETER   _____

PINTS   _____

PRESS   _____

Answers on page 91.

IN THE KNOW

How well-informed are you? Add IN to each word in the box to make a new word that fits one of the clues. IN can be added anywhere in the word—beginning, middle, or end. The first one has been done for you.

DEED	DOG	~~FAT~~	FORM
IMAGE	ME	MARES	MUTE
OK	POT	ROUTE	SIDE

1. Pass out   FAINT

2. Not yours   _____

3. Regular procedure   _____

4. Sharp end of a pencil   _____

5. Certainly!   _____

6. Pig's noise   _____

7. Accomplishing   _____

8. $1/60$ of an hour   _____

9. Sea soldiers   _____

10. Dream up   _____

11. Tell   _____

12. Not outdoors   _____

Answers on page 92.

HI THERE

Read each clue and fill in the letters to complete the answer word. Then write the letters with numbers under them in the same-numbered blanks below. Finally, read across to answer this riddle: What insect was asked to leave the rain forest?

Small mountain

H I __ __
    2

Between second and fourth

__ H I __ __
        7

Slapping

H I __ __ __ __ __
     4 5 3   10

Largest city in Illinois

__ H I __ __ __ __
        1

Home for buzzing insects

__ __ __ H I __ __
8   6

Hurrying

__ __ __ H I __ __
9

Answer: __   __ __ __ __ __ __ __ __ __
          1   2 3 4 5 6 7 8 9 10

FILM CLIP

Number the pictures from 1 to 8 to make a story without words.

Answer on page 87.

FOUR FITS

Place a four-letter word from the box into the blanks below to complete a word that fits the clue. All words in the box will be used.

ACHE	**DENT**	**EASE**	**EVER**	**FORM**
HAVE	**NOUN**	**PAST**	**RACE**	**TERM**

1. W A __ __ __ __ E L O N   summer fruit

2. B __ __ __ __ __ L O R   a man who isn't married

3. M I S B E __ __ __ __   act badly

4. B __ __ __ __ __ L E T   wrist jewelry

5. P E R __ __ __ __ __ E R   someone who acts in a show

6. P L __ __ __ __ __ D   very happy

7. A N __ __ __ __ __ C E R   commentator at sporting events

8. __ __ __ __ __ U R E   place where cows graze

9. A C C I __ __ __ __ __   unplanned event, like falling off a bike

10. R E T R I __ __ __ __ __   type of dog

Answers on page 93.

END OF THE LINE

Answer each clue with a five-letter word and write it in the blanks. Then read down the last column to answer this riddle: How do you make an egg laugh?

Random letters have been placed in some of the blanks as hints to help you along.

1. Intelligent
   __ M __ __ __

2. Hissing reptile
   __ __ __ K __

3. Tiny
   __ __ __ __ __

4. Round item on a necklace
   P __ __ __ __

5. Spicy dish made with beef, peppers, and beans
   __ __ __ __ I

6. Like sugar
   __ __ __ __ __

7. Spaghetti, macaroni, linguine, etc.
   __ __ S __ __

8. Opposite of late
   __ __ __ __ __

9. The state west of Wyoming
   I __ __ __ __

10. Desert animal with humps
    __ __ __ __ __

11. Speedy
    Q __ __ __ __

Answers on page 92.

RURAL EDUCATION

Cross off each word described in the clues. Then write the leftover words—from **RIGHT** to **LEFT** and **BOTTOM** to **TOP**—on the line. They won't make any sense. But . . . change just one letter in each word to find the answer to this riddle: What do farmers learn in school?

CLUES:

1. Four U.S. state capitals

2. Two anagrams of ALTER

3. Five birds

4. Three synonyms for FRIEND

5. Five bodies of water

6. Three end-of-year holidays

WRING	OCEAN	LATER	POND
PIGEON	FROG	PAL	PROVIDENCE
STREAM	RIVER	ALERT	BUDDY
CHRISTMAS	WOODPECKER	CHUM	PIPE
PIERRE	KWANZA	BELL	HAWK
DENVER	HANUKKAH	GO	PENGUIN
FALCON	LAKE	NOW	TOPEKA

Leftover words: _____

_____

Change one letter in each word: _____

_____

Answers on page 88.

WATCH DOG?

Find and circle the fourteen listed breeds of dogs in the grid. Look up, down, and diagonally, both forward and backward. Then, take the leftover letters from the grid and write them on the line from left to right and top to bottom to answer this riddle: What should a dog do when it wants to stop a DVD player?

For an extra challenge, you'll need to figure out where the spaces go between the words in the answer phrase.

BEAGLE	GRIFFON
BOXER	PEKINGESE
COLLIE	PUG
CORGI	SALUKI
DACHSHUND	SAMOYED
GREAT DANE	SPANIEL
GREYHOUND	TERRIER

T	G	R	E	A	T	D	A	N	E
P	E	N	O	F	F	I	R	G	S
D	I	R	R	E	I	L	E	R	E
E	L	S	R	G	E	S	X	E	G
Y	L	T	R	I	H	E	O	Y	N
O	O	O	N	K	E	P	B	H	I
M	C	A	A	U	W	R	G	O	K
A	P	S	B	L	U	T	T	U	E
S	E	L	G	A	E	B	O	N	P
D	A	C	H	S	H	U	N	D	N

Answer: _____

Answers on page 93.

BEFORE OR AFTER

Find a riddle and its answer by changing each letter below to the one that comes **BEFORE** *OR* **AFTER** it in the alphabet. Use this guide to help you make your choices.

A B C D E F G H I J K L M N O P Q R S T U V W X Y Z

X G Z   C P   U F B B G D S R   V D B Q

_____

T T O F K B T R D T?

_____

A F D B T R F   U G F H Q   R U V C D M S T

_____

B Q F   R N   C S J H G S.

_____

Now, do the same thing again to find another riddle and answer.

VGBU EP RQJCDQT FBS VHSI

UGDJS IBLCTQFFQT?

GQFMDI GKHDR.

Answers on page 88.

CROSS AND DOWN

Figure out which two letters are missing from each answer and write them in the blanks to form a word that answers the clue. Then read **DOWN** the lines, two letters at a time, to find the answer to this riddle: Why did the kid **CROSS** the playground?

1. The tenth month   O C _ _ B E R

2. Doctor who operates   S U R _ _ O N

3. Popular fabric for clothes   C O _ _ O N

4. Type of control for a TV   R E M _ _ E

5. Place for watching movies   T _ _ A T E R

6. Type of cheese   C _ _ T A G E

7. Sandy areas   B E A C _ _ S

8. Needing water   T H I _ _ T Y

9. Yummy!   D E _ _ C I O U S

10. Pupil   S T U _ _ N T

Answers on page 93.

FOR THE BIRDS

Count the number of letters in each bird word below and then place it in the right spot in the grid, ignoring any spaces between words. When the grid is full, read down one of the columns to find the name of another bird. Each word fits one spot only.

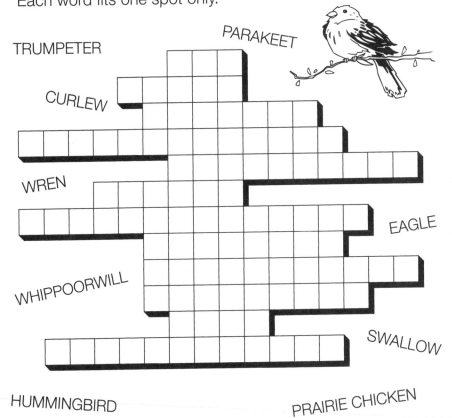

PARAKEET

TRUMPETER

CURLEW

WREN

EAGLE

WHIPPOORWILL

SWALLOW

HUMMINGBIRD

PRAIRIE CHICKEN

WOODPECKER

JAY

TURKEY VULTURE

Answers on page 96.

SQUISH/SQUASH

Two related items are squished together on each line. All the letters in each word are in the correct order; you just have to separate them.

Example: F I T W F E N T E E N T Y = FIFTEEN & TWENTY

The hints on this page list the categories for each set of squished words, but they're in random order!

HINTS

AREAS IN A SCHOOL

COLORS

FACE PARTS

FLOWERS

HALLOWEEN COSTUMES

ICE CREAM FLAVORS

SPORTS

STORMS

U. S. CITIES

VEGGIES

1. BASKHOCETBAKEYLL

   _____ & _____

2. ROTUSELISPS

   _____ & _____

3. SPCABINACBAHGE

   _____ & _____

4. CHIATLCAGANOTA

   _____ & _____

5. GREPURENPLE

   _____ & _____

6. GYHAMLL

   _____ & _____

7. HCYUCLRRIONECANE

   _____ & _____

8. EMOYEUBRTOWSH

   _____ & _____

9. PIVASTANILCHIOLA

   _____ & _____

10. WIGHOTCHST

   _____ & _____

Answers on page 93.

DIZZY DEFINITIONS

Match the words in the left column with the dizzy definitions in the right column. Don't think of the real meaning of the words. Instead, break down each word into two parts.

Example: HERRING = the girl's jewelry (her + ring)

1. ALLOWING	**A.** dad leases
2. BROOMSTICK	**B.** country made of fish parts
3. HOURGLASS	**C.** skinny royal guy
4. FINLAND	**D.** tiny chess piece
5. FORGIVING	**E.** 60-minute window
6. CARAWAY	**F.** cleaning tools make clock sounds
7. MANAGED	**G.** in favor of charity
8. PARENTS	**H.** auto's gone
9. THINKING	**I.** guy got older
10. WEEKNIGHT	**J.** everyone has bills to pay

Answers on page 91.

MEMORY QUIZ

Study this page for 60 seconds. Then turn to the next page to answer the questions and see how much you remember.

56

How many questions can you answer about the scene on the previous page? No looking back!

1. What is written below the bike sign?

_____

2. What's the name of the street?

_____

3. Does the kid's tricycle have a basket?

_____

4. Is anyone jogging?

_____

5. Is it raining?

_____

6. How many dogs are being walked?

_____

7. What number is on the skateboarder's shirt?

_____

8. How many people are wearing headphones?

_____

Answers on page 93.

DOUBLE-ACTING WORDS

One word will answer each set of clues. Write the double-acting word in the blank space.

Example: National bird of the U.S.A.
+ type of Boy Scout = **Answer:** ___EAGLE___

1. Champion golfer ___ Woods
   + striped animal = _____

2. Cooling device + supporter of the team = _____

3. Someone who fights in a ring
   + dog with a short square face = _____

4. Baseball player who throws the ball
   + a container for pouring drinks = _____

5. Stuffed animal (___ bear)
   + nickname for Theodore Roosevelt = _____

6. Bottom part of a foot + fish, filet of ___ = _____

7. Tool for changing a tire
   + a picture card in a deck = _____

8. Noise made by a dog
   + outer covering of a tree = _____

9. Honest and just + large county event = _____

10. Twinkler in the night sky
    + lead actor or actress in a movie = _____

Answers on page 89.

IT'S NOT WHAT YOU SAY . . .

. . . It's how you say it. Each box contains words and/or letters that create coded messages. Look at the size of the words, the direction they're facing, and other visual clues to figure out the real expressions.

Example: EHCA = backache

1.

BEND
SDRAW

_____

2.

speed   speed   speed   speed   speed

                                              bike

speed   speed   speed   speed   speed

_____

3. BO   NE

_____

4.

SLEEP
PARTY

_____

5.

S P L O S T A C E

_____

6.

BROTHER

7.

T
O
E
A
R
T
H

8.

ME   REPEAT

_____

9.

READ

_____

10.

```
        S
        K
        I
        I
COUNTRY
        G
```

_____

Answers on page 94.

GIRLS, GIRLS, GIRLS

Put each girl's name in the grid. Start with the given letters and work from there until the grid is complete.

3 Letters
EVE
KAY
KIM
MEG

4 Letters
IRIS
JOAN
MARY
MONA
ROSE

5 Letters
AMBER
ANGIE
EMILY
JENNA
KELLY
LINDA
NANCY
SARAH

6 Letters
ANDREA
LESLEY
SOPHIA
YVONNE

7 Letters
ANNETTE
BRIANNA
MADISON
MARILYN

Answers on page 95.

OPPOSITE DISTRACTION

Think of a word that's the opposite of the word in the column on the left. Write it in the blank spaces to form a new word that answers the clue on the right. Then copy the numbered letters to the blanks below that have the same numbers to answer this riddle: Why did the horse sneeze?

Begin	P R E T __ __ __ 12 5	Make believe
Healthy	G R __ __ __ E D 1 11 7	Cooked on a barbecue
Him	S __ __ __ I F F 3	Law-enforcement officer
Go	W E L __ __ __ __ 13	Greet on arrival
Early	R E __ __ __ __ D 15 4 2	Connected by ancestry
Good	__ __ __ M I N T O N 6	Game played with rackets
Bottom	O C __ __ __ U S 16 14	Eight-armed creature
First	P __ __ __ __ I C 9	Synthetic material
Stand	V I __ __ __ O R 8 10	Guest

__ __   __ __ __   __   __ __ __ __ __ __ __   __ __ __ __
1 2   3 4 5   6   7 8 9 10 11 12   13 14 15 16

Answers on page 94.

OOPS!

Use this code to find a riddle and its answer.

A = 1	H = 8	O = 15	V = 22
B = 2	I = 9	P = 16	W = 23
C = 3	J = 10	Q = 17	X = 24
D = 4	K = 11	R = 18	Y = 25
E = 5	L = 12	S = 19	Z = 26
F = 6	M = 13	T = 20	
G = 7	N = 14	U = 21	

23 8 1 20   9 19   12 1 18 7 5   1 14 4   7 18 1 25

_____

1 14 4   7 15 5 19   1 18 15 21 14 4   1 14 4

_____

1 18 15 21 14 4   9 14   3 9 18 3 12 5 19?

_____

1 14   5 12 5 16 8 1 14 20   19 20 21 3 11   9 14   1

_____

18 5 22 15 12 22 9 14 7   4 15 15 18.

_____

Answer on page 91.

SOCCER SPRINT

Oh, no! Someone left his soccer equipment in his gym locker. Can you move him through the maze quickly so he can pick up his gear before the game starts?

Answers on page 93.

SOME DIFFERENCE

Circle ten differences between the picture on this page and the picture on the opposite page.

Answers on page 92.

SLIGHT CHANGE

In the puzzles below, the underlined letter in each word needs to be changed to form a riddle and answer that make sense. One has been done to get you started.

Example:

THAT GO SOU GO WISH I GLUE SHALE?

What do you do with a blue whale?

SHEER AT US.

Cheer it up.

1. WHIT AS TOE TEST THINK NO PET ON I TIE?

_____

SOUR TENTH.

_____

2. NOW GOES I SLOWER TIDE I LIKE?

_____

AT RUSHES INS METALS.

_____

3. WH<u>O</u> DI<u>M</u> TH<u>Y</u> <u>P</u>AN S<u>T</u>EEP U<u>D</u>DER HA<u>S</u> <u>T</u>AR?

_____

H<u>I</u> WA<u>S</u>TED <u>N</u>O <u>T</u>AKE US <u>L</u>ILY <u>IT</u> <u>S</u>HE MO<u>A</u>NING.

_____

4. W<u>R</u>Y <u>H</u>AS <u>S</u>HE P<u>I</u>T <u>B</u>IG CALLE<u>R</u> IN<u>N</u>?

_____

<u>IS</u> <u>W</u>EPT <u>S</u>UNNING O<u>A</u>T <u>I</u>F T<u>I</u>E <u>M</u>EN.

_____

5. <u>T</u>HAT <u>G</u>O TR<u>I</u>ES LI<u>M</u>E <u>S</u>O <u>B</u>RINK?

_____

ROO<u>M</u> <u>D</u>EER.

_____

Answers on page 94.

SO BOSSY

The word in the right column uses all the letters of the word in the left column EXCEPT for one letter. Write the missing letter in the blank. Then write the letters in the same-numbered blanks below to reveal a phrase that describes what people do when they boss other people around.

ALERTING	___	(3)	TEARING
THEATERS	___	(6)	RETASTE
CHAIRMEN	___	(1)	MACHINE
TEACHERS	___	(11)	CHEATER
ORIENTAL	___	(8)	TOENAIL
FOURTEEN	___	(7)	FORTUNE
HUNGRIER	___	(2)	HERRING
TOURISTS	___	(12)	SUITORS
MODELING	___	(9)	MINGLED
ORDERING	___	(10)	GRINDER
STRANGER	___	(5)	RANGERS
COSTUMES	___	(4)	CUSTOMS

___ ___ ___ ___   ___ ___ ___   ___ ___ ___ ___ ___
1   2   3   4   5   6   7   8   9   10 11 12

Answer on page 95.

CHANGE OVER

Each word in the list can be an anagram. An anagram is a word that, with the letters rearranged, spells an entirely different word, for example DEAF and FADE. Rearrange the letters in each word in the list below to create a new word and then write it in the grid. When all the new words are in the grid, read down the starred column to find a place where people are always changing.

1. DEAF
2. WORTH
3. WAKE
4. VOTES
5. SHOUT
6. QUITE
7. THIN
8. GAPE
9. CHARM
10. CORK
11. BORE
12. MILE

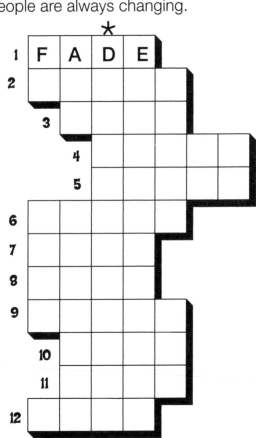

Answers on page 96.

HEALTH TIP

Answer each clue. Then write the letters in the matching blanks in the box below to get a riddle and answer.

CLUES

1. Very small

$\overline{~}$ $\overline{~}$ $\overline{~}$ $\overline{~}$
4 18 23 7

2. Not dry

$\overline{~}$ $\overline{~}$ $\overline{~}$
12 24 34

3. Place with caged animals

$\overline{~}$ $\overline{~}$ $\overline{~}$
26 8 35

4. Formal wedding dress

$\overline{~}$ $\overline{~}$ $\overline{~}$ $\overline{~}$
29 32 40 20

5. Despise

$\overline{~}$ $\overline{~}$ $\overline{~}$ $\overline{~}$
2 19 37 25

6. Opposite of night

$\overline{~}$ $\overline{~}$ $\overline{~}$
5 16 42

7. Whole ___ bread

$\overline{~}$ $\overline{~}$ $\overline{~}$ $\overline{~}$ $\overline{~}$
1 38 14 41 21

8. Animal, billy_____

$\overline{~}$ $\overline{~}$ $\overline{~}$ $\overline{~}$
17 6 3 31

9. The earth revolves around this

$\overline{~}$ $\overline{~}$ $\overline{~}$
28 33 15

10. Home

$\overline{~}$ $\overline{~}$ $\overline{~}$ $\overline{~}$ $\overline{~}$
13 11 9 22 39

11. Nourish (rhymes with seed)

$\overline{~}$ $\overline{~}$ $\overline{~}$ $\overline{~}$
36 27 30 10

— — — —   — —   — — —   — —
1 2 3 4   5 6   7 8 9   10 11

— — —   — —   — — — — —
12 13 14   15 16   17 18 19 20 21

— — — — — — —?
22 23 24 25 26 27 28

— — —   — — —   — —   — — —   — — —.
29 30 31   32 33 34   35 36   37 38 39   40 41 42

Answers on page 92.

STUFF IT!

Take a word from the box and stuff it between two letters of a word on the list to form a new word that answers the clue. Example: "SAG" stuffed in between the R and E in the word "CORE" makes "CORSAGE" (small bouquet worn on a wrist or shoulder).

ALL	**RAG**
EGG	**STAR**
FOR	**THE**
ONE	**US**
OUT	**USE**

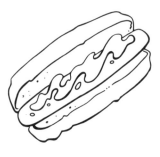

1. BEE   (opposite of after) _____
2. SHED   (yelled) _____
3. FAR   (male parent) _____
4. SHOW   (like water in a wading pool) _____
5. MUM   (place for paintings and sculpture) _____
6. BAR   (person who asks for money) _____
7. COIN   (a relative) _____
8. FILE   (easily broken) _____
9. MUD   (condiment used on hot dogs) _____
10. PIERS   (people who settle into new areas) _____

Answers on page 86.

PLAY BALL

Circle the two pictures that are exactly alike.

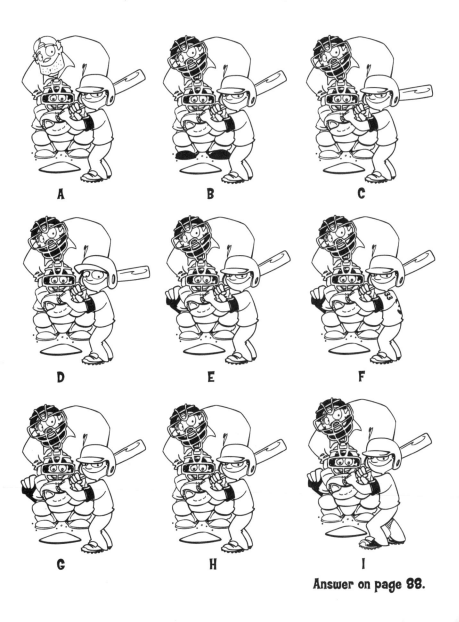

A

B

C

D

E

F

G

H

I

Answer on page 88.

EASY WIN

Find and circle the nineteen weather-related words in the list. Look up, down, and diagonally, both forward and backward. Then take the leftover letters from the grid and read them from left to right and top to bottom to answer this riddle: What did the weatherman say when he won a race?

For an extra challenge, you'll need to figure out where the spaces go between the words in the answer phrase.

CLOUD

CYCLONE

DRIZZLE

FLURRY

FOG

GALE

HAIL

HAZE

HEAT

HUMIDITY

LIGHTNING

RAIN

SHOWER

SLEET

SQUALL

STORM

THUNDER

TWISTER

WIND

M	F	T	D	H	A	H	E	A	T
R	L	S	U	H	G	U	T	G	H
O	U	L	O	A	W	M	N	A	U
T	R	E	L	Z	Z	I	R	D	N
S	R	E	C	E	N	D	N	S	D
Q	Y	T	W	T	S	I	U	C	E
U	H	A	H	O	W	T	A	B	R
A	R	G	E	A	H	Y	E	R	Z
L	I	O	T	W	I	S	T	E	R
L	E	F	E	N	O	L	C	Y	C

Answer: _____

TRIPLE TREAT

Separate the word list below into three categories: Drinks, Fruits, and Veggies. Then write the words in the grids in the spaces where they fit best. Each grid will only contain words from one category. A few letters have already been placed to get you started.

APPLE	JUICE	PEACH
APRICOT	LEMONADE	PEPPER
BANANA	LETTUCE	PLUM
BEAN	LIMEADE	RADISH
CELERY	MILK	SPINACH
CHERRY	MOCHA	TANGERINE
CIDER	MUSHROOM	TEA
COCOA	ONION	WATER
CORN	ORANGE	
EGGNOG	PAPAYA	

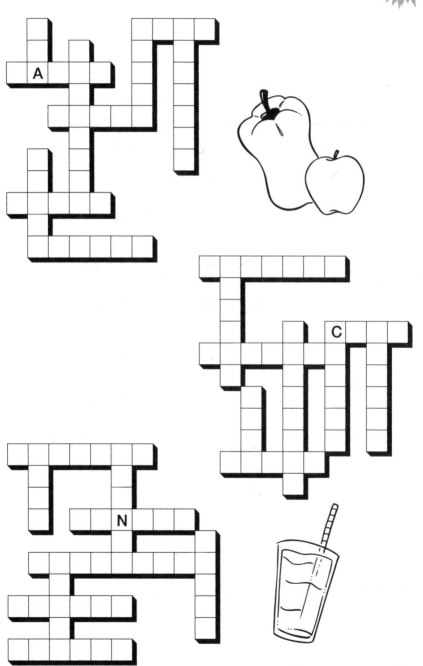

Answers on page 96.

GOOD SPORTS

Write the nine scattered words on the grid horizontally and in alphabetical order. Then read the circled letters from left to right and top to bottom to answer this riddle: Why are waiters and waitresses good at tennis?

SLOWEST

SHOUTED

SHALLOW

SEEKING

STAPLER

SURVIVE

SCENERY

SPONGES

SATCHEL

Answers on page 94.

SANDWICH FILLINGS

Place a filling in the middle of each sandwich and then read downward for a tasty lunch of seven letter words.

TURKEY SALAMI TOMATO SALMON CHEESE

B M R L V H
I A E I E O
S C S C S N

_ _ _ _ _ _

U I R N E S
I N V S L T
T E E E S Y

H P M C I A
I Y I H N V
M R L I D E

_ _ _ _ _ _

E M I N O U
L I O E R E
F D N Y S S

F R S B A P
A E H O L L
N G O O L A

_ _ _ _ _ _

A L T L R P
S A E E G E
Y R N T Y N

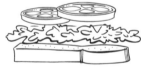

P E F P M H
L Q E I A O
A U E R M L

_ _ _ _ _ _

T L I T A D
I L N E L A
C Y G S S Y

F C P I C S
O O R N A C
R C O F P H

_ _ _ _ _ _

U N O N A O
N U T T I L
E T E S N S

Answers on page 95.

GARDEN GOOFS

Circle the nine things that are wrong here.

Answers on page 85.

STEP BY STEP ... AGAIN

To find a riddle and its answer, start at the circled letter in the grid and move one square at a time. Go straight across, up, or down, but *not* diagonally. Write each letter in the blanks to the right of the grid, and then cross it off in the grid. All letters and symbols in the grid will be used once.

I	E	H	T
R	S	A	N
D	A	L	O
?	M	A	T
-	O	Y	U
N	E	I	P
S	H	G	S
.	R	S	E
H	O	A	H
O	D	T	(W)

W _ _ _   _ _

_ _ _ _ _ _   _ _ _

_ _   _ _ _ _ _   _

_ _ _ _ _?

_ _ _ _ _-_ _ _ _ _ _ _.

Answers on page 86.

TEE TIME

There wasn't enough space to write out the first and last names of famous people from the past on these T-shirts—there was room for only three letters on each line. The letters on the top line indicate the person's first name; the letters below are part of the last name. Can you name all these people? Use the random hints to guide you.

Example: __ARK is MARK

__WAI__ is TWAIN

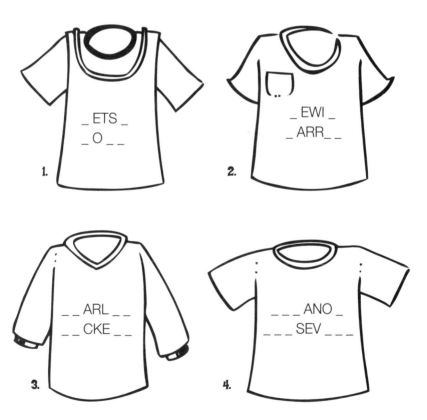

1. _ ETS _
   _ O _ _

2. _ EWI _
   _ ARR _ _

3. _ _ ARL _ _
   _ _ CKE _ _

4. _ _ _ ANO _
   _ _ _ SEV _ _ _

HINTS

Alice in Wonderland creator
A Christmas Carol author
Father of our country
Female pilot
Midnight rider
Moon walker

First Lady married to the 32nd U.S. president
Woman who sewed the first U.S. flag
Female Nobel Prize winner
Red Cross founder

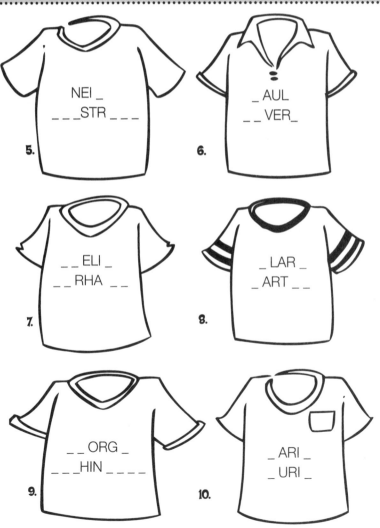

5. NEI _
   _ _ _STR _ _ _

6. _ AUL
   _ _ VER_

7. _ _ ELI _
   _ _ RHA _ _

8. _ LAR _
   _ ART _ _

9. _ _ ORG _
   _ _ _HIN _ _ _ _

10. _ ARI _
    _ URI _

Answers on page 96.

YUMMY!

Count the number of letters in each dessert below
and then place the dessert in the right spot in the grid,
ignoring any spacing between words. When the grid is
full, read down one of the columns to find a special treat.
Each word fits in one spot only.

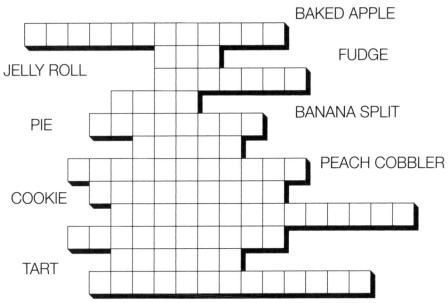

BAKED APPLE

FUDGE

JELLY ROLL

BANANA SPLIT

PIE

PEACH COBBLER

COOKIE

TART

ICE CREAM SUNDAE

FROZEN CUSTARD

BROWNIE

DOUGHNUT

Answers on page 96.

ANSWERS

OPTICAL CONFUSION (pg. 5)

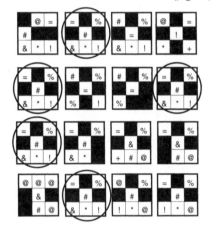

THIS AUTO BE FUN (pg. 9)

RT1

1OSNE1

H&EMAN

W8R

CCAP1O

RZNKIDS

LAZY BONES (pg. 10)

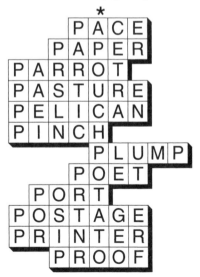

Answer: A pouch potato.

GARDEN GOOFS (pg. 80)

FOOD FIGHT (pg. 16)

STEP BY STEP ... AGAIN
(pg. 81)

WHAT DO HORSES PUT ON THEIR SALAD?
    MAYO-NEIGHS.

MAGIC SQUARES (pg. 12)

A

S	H	U	T
H	O	P	E
U	P	O	N
T	E	N	T

B

S	I	C	K
I	R	O	N
C	O	N	E
K	N	E	W

C

P	L	A	Y
L	O	S	E
A	S	I	A
Y	E	A	R

D

C	A	S	H
A	R	E	A
S	E	L	L
H	A	L	F

THE NAME GAME (pg. 7)

1. FRA**GILE**
2. B**LOUSE**
3. P**LENTY**
4. L**ABEL**
5. CARA**MEL**
6. WEEK**END**
7. SE**SAME**
8. MI**RACLE**
9. **BENE**ATH
10. **DANGE**ROUS

STUFF IT! (pg. 72)

1. BE**FORE**
2. SH**OUTED**
3. FA**THER**
4. SH**ALLOW**
5. M**USEUM**
6. BE**GGAR**
7. COUSIN
8. **FRA**GILE
9. MU**STARD**
10. PI**ONEERS**

TEACHER'S PET (pg. 14)

1. FLY
2. VIRUS
3. STOMACH
4. LATECOMER
5. STRESS
6. CONCLUSION
7. BATTLE
8. GOBBLED
9. EARTHLING
10. STRANGE
11. RODEO
12. EXTRA
13. AWARD
14. COUCH
15. VACUUM
16. WALTZ

Leftover words: POTS IF FLOOD RESTS.
Answer: LOTS OF BLOOD TESTS.

FRONT OF THE LINE (pg. 6)

<u>H</u>ELLO
<u>E</u>IGHT

<u>W</u>OMEN
<u>A</u>PRIL
<u>S</u>ALAD

<u>T</u>RICK
<u>I</u>RONS
<u>P</u>LATE
<u>P</u>EACE
<u>E</u>ARTH
<u>D</u>UCKS

ADD-A-LETTER (pg. 8)

A
M A
A R M
M A R S
M A R E S
S T R E A M
H A M S T E R

FILM CLIP (pg. 40)

RURAL EDUCATION (pg. 44)

A. PROVIDENCE, PIERRE, DENVER, TOPEKA
B. LATER, ALERT
C. PIGEON, WOODPECKER, HAWK, PENGUIN, FALCON
D. PAL, BUDDY, CHUM
E. OCEAN, POND, STREAM, RIVER, LAKE
F. CHRISTMAS, KWANZA, HANUKKAH

Leftover words: Now go bell pipe frog wring.
Answer: How to tell ripe from wrong.

A-MAZE-ING PATH (pg. 23)

PLAY BALL (pg. 73)

E and G are the same.

DUMB THUMB (pg. 19)

1. BOAT COAT
2. CANE LANE
3. SPRING RING
4. MOUSE HOUSE
5. PORK FORK
6. RUG BUG
7. GRAY CLAY
8. GOOD WOOD
9. TEN MEN
10. FUNNY BUNNY

Story: The **funny bunny** put on a **boat coat** and a **spring ring** and walked down the **cane lane** to the **mouse house,** which was made of **gray clay** and **good wood**. There he saw **ten men** hoping to use a **pork fork** on a baked ham. Unfortunately, the **rug bug** had already finished it!

BEFORE OR AFTER (pg. 48)

WHY DO TEACHERS WEAR SUNGLASSES?
    BECAUSE THEIR STUDENTS ARE SO BRIGHT.
WHAT DO SPIDERS EAT WITH THEIR HAMBURGERS?
    FRENCH FLIES.

AUTHOR! AUTHOR! (pg. 31)

Car Talk by Otto Moe Bill
Don't Cross at the Green!
   by J. Walker
Making Better Sandwiches
   by May O. Naze
Mexican Food by K. C. Dilla
Math Made Easy by Cal Q.
Later
I Confess by Gil Tee
Cold State by Al Asker
No One Special by N. E. Buddy
Soft Lights by Ken Dell Styx
Genius at Work by A. Braine

THE "A" LIST (pg. 18)

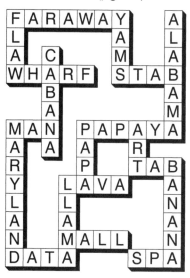

BODY LANGUAGE (pg. 20)

1. <u>LEG</u>END
2. PHAR<u>MACY</u>
3. POP<u>EYE</u>
4. T<u>EAR</u>ING
5. STAR<u>SHIP</u>
6. S<u>LIP</u>PERS
7. POTA<u>TOES</u>

RIDDLE CROSSWORD
(pg. 24)

Answer: Can I do the filling?

DOUBLE-ACTING WORDS
(pg. 57)

1. TIGER
2. FAN
3. BOXER
4. PITCHER
5. TEDDY
6. SOLE
7. JACK
8. BARK
9. FAIR
10. STAR

90

VACATION SPOT (pg. 21)

T<u>U</u>RNIP
RADIS<u>H</u>
L<u>EE</u>K

CEL<u>E</u>RY
P<u>E</u>PPER
CARRO<u>T</u>
AR<u>T</u>ICHOKE
SQ<u>U</u>ASH
<u>C</u>AULIFLOWER
CABBAG<u>E</u>

ON<u>I</u>ON
COR<u>N</u>
SPI<u>N</u>ACH

Answer: The Lettuce Inn

SOUND OFF (pg. 28)

1. HYMN
2. WOULD
3. MISSED
4. ROSE
5. EIGHT
6. CHEWS
7. DAZE
8. SWEET
9. THRONE
10. WHERE
11. MADE

Answer: Mum's the word

WHR HV LL TH VWLS GN? (pg. 30)

1. THE UGLY DUCKLING
2. CINDERELLA
3. THE LITTLE MERMAID
4. SLEEPING BEAUTY
5. RUMPELSTILTSKIN
6. BEAUTY AND THE BEAST
7. RAPUNZEL
8. THE EMPEROR'S NEW CLOTHES
9. SNOW WHITE
10. HANSEL AND GRETEL

EMERGENCY! (pg. 26)

1. HOUSE
2. ATE
3. MAIL
4. BACK
5. TOAST
6. GOAT
7. CHIPS
8. HELP
9. NINE
10. DIG
11. WHO

Answer: How does a sick pig get to the hospital? In a ham-bulance.

HI THERE (pg. 39)

HI<u>LL</u>
THIR<u>D</u>
H<u>I</u>T<u>T</u>ING
CHIC<u>AGO</u>
B<u>EE</u>HI<u>VE</u>
<u>R</u>USHIN<u>G</u>

Answer: A litterbug.

PICTURE CROSSWORD (pg. 34)

DIZZY DEFINITIONS (pg. 54)

1 – J	6 – H
2 – F	7 – I
3 – E	8 – A
4 – B	9 – C
5 – G	10 – D

CATCH OF THE DAY (pg. 29)

1. SON	7. FOR
2. MET	8. HIM
3. BLUSH	9. TON
4. PAN	10. SAT
5. COAL	11. HUT
6. SAD	12. TUB

CLOSE RELATIVES (pg. 36)

1. DINNER
   SUPPER
   BRUNCH

2. SHOES
   BOOTS
   SANDALS

3. MOTHER
   FATHER
   SISTER

4. LAKE
   RIVER
   POND

5. EYES
   EARS
   NOSE

6. TABLE
   CHAIR
   COUCH

7. STEAK
   VEAL
   PORK

8. TEA
   MILK
   SODA

9. SIX
   EIGHT
   FIVE

10. SWEATER
    PANTS
    DRESS

STEP BY STEP (pg. 22)

What holds water but is full of holes? A sponge.

DEAL ME OUT (pg. 32)

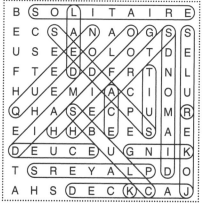

Answer: Because of the cheetahs.

OOPS! (pg. 62)

WHAT IS LARGE AND GRAY AND GOES AROUND AND AROUND IN CIRCLES?

AN ELEPHANT STUCK IN A REVOLVING DOOR.

IN THE KNOW (pg. 38)

1.	FAINT	7.	DOING
2.	MINE	8.	MINUTE
3.	ROUTINE	9.	MARINES
4.	POINT	10.	IMAGINE
5.	INDEED	11.	INFORM
6.	OINK	12.	INSIDE

HEALTH TIP (pg. 70)

1.	TINY	7.	WHEAT
2.	WET	8.	GOAT
3.	ZOO	9.	SUN
4.	GOWN	10.	HOUSE
5.	HATE	11.	FEED
6.	DAY		

Answer: What do you do when a giant sneezes? Get out of the way.

END OF THE LINE (pg. 43)

1. SMAR<u>T</u>
2. SNAK<u>E</u>
3. SMAL<u>L</u>
4. PEAR<u>L</u>

5. CHIL<u>I</u>
6. SWEE<u>T</u>

7. PAST<u>A</u>

8. EARL<u>Y</u>
9. IDAH<u>O</u>
10. CAME<u>L</u>
11. QUIC<u>K</u>

Answer: Tell it a yolk.

SOME DIFFERENCE (pg. 64)

WATCH DOG? (pg. 46)

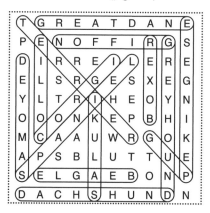

Answer: Press the paws button.

FOUR FITS (pg. 42)

1. WA<u>TERME</u>LON
2. B<u>ACHE</u>LOR
3. MISBE<u>HAVE</u>
4. B<u>RACE</u>LET
5. PER<u>FORME</u>R
6. PL<u>EASE</u>D
7. AN<u>NOUNC</u>ER
8. <u>PAST</u>URE
9. ACCI<u>DENT</u>
10. RETRI<u>EVER</u>

MEMORY QUIZ (pgs. 55–56)

1. SHARE THE ROAD
2. ELM STREET
3. YES
4. YES
5. NO
6. TWO
7. THE NUMBER 8
8. TWO

CROSS AND DOWN (pg. 50)

1. OC<u>TO</u>BER
2. SUR<u>GEO</u>N
3. CO<u>TT</u>ON
4. REM<u>OTE</u>
5. T<u>HEA</u>TER
6. CO<u>TT</u>AGE
7. BEAC<u>HES</u>
8. THI<u>RS</u>TY
9. DEL<u>I</u>CIOUS
10. STU<u>DENT</u>

Answer: To get to the other slide.

SOCCER SPRINT (pg. 63)

SQUISH/SQUASH (pg. 52)

1. Basketball & hockey
2. Roses & tulips
3. Spinach & cabbage
4. Chicago & Atlanta
5. Green & purple
6. Gym & hall
7. Hurricane & cyclone
8. Eyebrows & mouth
9. Pistachio & vanilla
10. Witch & ghost

OPPOSITE DISTRACTION

(pg. 61)

PRET<u>END</u>
GR<u>ILL</u>ED
<u>SH</u>ERIFF
WEL<u>COME</u>
RE<u>LATED</u>
<u>BAD</u>MINTON
OC<u>TOP</u>US
P<u>LAS</u>TIC
VI<u>SIT</u>OR

Answer: It had a little colt.

SLIGHT CHANGE (pg. 66)

1. WHAT IS THE BEST THING
   TO PUT IN A PIE?
   YOUR TEETH.
2. HOW DOES A FLOWER
   RIDE A BIKE?
   IT PUSHES ITS PETALS.
3. WHY DID THE MAN SLEEP
   UNDER HIS CAR?
   HE WANTED TO WAKE UP
   OILY IN THE MORNING.
4. WHY WAS THE PET PIG
   CALLED INK?
   IT KEPT RUNNING OUT OF
   THE PEN.
5. WHAT DO TREES LIKE TO
   DRINK?
   ROOT BEER.

IT'S NOT WHAT YOU SAY ...

(pg. 58)

1. BEND OVER
   BACKWARDS
2. TEN-SPEED BIKE
3. BROKEN BONE
4. SLEEPOVER PARTY
5. LOST IN SPACE
6. BIG BROTHER
7. DOWN TO EARTH
8. REPEAT AFTER ME
9. READ BETWEEN THE
   LINES
10. CROSS-COUNTRY
    SKIING

GOOD SPORTS (pg. 78)

S	A	T	C	H	E	L
S	C	E	N	E	R	Y
S	E	E	K	I	N	G
S	H	A	L	L	O	W
S	H	O	U	T	E	D
S	L	O	W	E	S	T
S	P	O	N	G	E	S
S	T	A	P	L	E	R
S	U	R	V	I	V	E

Answer: They know how to
serve.

GIRLS, GIRLS, GIRLS (pg. 60)

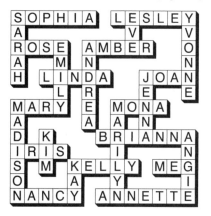

EASY WIN (pg. 74)

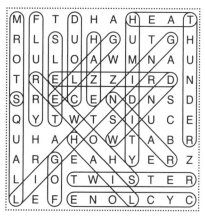

Answer: That was such a breeze.

SANDWICH FILLINGS (pg. 79)

```
B M R L V H      F R S B A P
I A E I E O      A E H O L L
S C S C S N      N G O O L A
C H E E S E      T U R K E Y
U I R N E S      A L T L R P
I N V S L T      S A E E G E
T E E E S Y      Y R N T Y N

        H P M C I A
        I Y I H N V
        M R L I D E
        S A L M O N
        E M I N O U
        L I O E R E
        F D N Y S S

P E F P M H      F C P I C S
L Q E I A O      O O R N A C
A U E R M L      R C O F P H
S A L A M I      T O M A T O
T L I T A D      U N O N A O
I L N E L A      N U T T I L
C Y G S S Y      E T E S N S
```

SO BOSSY (pg. 68)

ALERTING	L	TEARING
THEATERS	H	RETASTE
CHAIRMEN	R	MACHINE
TEACHERS	S	CHEATER
ORIENTAL	R	TOENAIL
FOURTEEN	E	FORTUNE
HUNGRIER	U	HERRING
TOURISTS	T	SUITORS
MODELING	O	MINGLED
ORDERING	O	GRINDER
STRANGER	T	RANGERS
COSTUMES	E	CUSTOMS

Answer: Rule the roost

CHANGE OVER (pg. 69)

```
F A D E*
T H R O W
  W E A K
    S T O V E
    S O U T H
Q U I E T
H I N T
P A G E
M A R C H
  R O C K
  R O B E
  L I M E
```

Answer: Dressing room

TEE TIME (pg. 82)

1. Betsy Ross
2. Lewis Carroll
3. Charles Dickens
4. Eleanor Roosevelt
5. Neil Armstrong
6. Paul Revere
7. Amelia Earhart
8. Clara Barton
9. George Washington
10. Marie Curie

YUMMY! (pg. 84)

Answer: Birthday cake

TRIPLE TREAT (pg. 76)

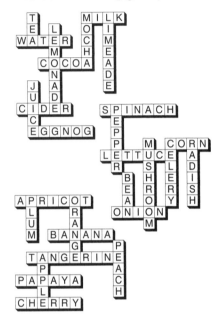

FOR THE BIRDS (pg. 51)

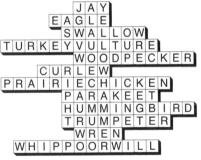

Answer: Yellowhammer